CONDEMNED
TO MEANING

———

The John Dewey Society Lecture is delivered annually under the sponsorship of the John Dewey Society at the annual meeting of the National Society of College Teachers of Education. Arrangements for the presentation and publication of the Lecture are under the direction of the John Dewey Society Commission on Lectures.

ARTHUR G. WIRTH, Washington University, St. Louis, Missouri
Chairman and Editor

ARCHIBALD ANDERSON
University of Illinois
R. FREEMAN BUTTS
Teachers College
Columbia University

HAROLD SHANE
University of Indiana
WILLIAM O. STANLEY
University of Illinois

THE JOHN DEWEY SOCIETY LECTURESHIP — NUMBER SEVEN

CONDEMNED TO MEANING

by

HUSTON SMITH

PROFESSOR OF PHILOSOPHY
MASSACHUSETTS INSTITUTE OF TECHNOLOGY

FOREWORD BY

Arthur G. Wirth

CHAIRMAN, THE JOHN DEWEY SOCIETY
COMMISSION ON PUBLICATIONS

HARPER & ROW, PUBLISHERS

NEW YORK, EVANSTON, AND LONDON

For Karen, Gael, and Kimberly

Contents

Foreword

by

ARTHUR G. WIRTH,

CHAIRMAN, COMMISSION ON LECTURES,

The John Dewey Society For the Study of Education and Culture

John Dewey argued that philosophy's office is to function in the arena of man's experience. It should shun the temptation to take shelter in the reiteration of past pronouncements or to confine itself to esoteric concerns of campus seminars. When men are bewildered by the shock of revolutionary change, philosophy should speak to their urgent problems. If it remains alive, it must be part of the history of its time, but with a responsibility to bring to the level of consciousness concerns that are disturbing, so that men may have a chance to act on them.

Professor Huston Smith in *Condemned to Meaning* works in the spirit of that injunction. His effort fits the purpose of the John Dewey Lecture Series, which is to help us see the work of the teaching profession in fresh perspective. He asks us to consider the case that the problem of life-meaning now has an urgency that demands the attention of philosophers and educators alike.

In the modern era, a major task has been to crack the cake of custom that restricted man from realizing his full humanity. That fight had to be waged. It still must be fought in a thousand

times and places to free men from ancient bonds and oppres-
sions. But the second half of the twentieth century sees intellectual, technological, and social revolutions far advanced. In
their wake lie shattered husks of traditions and ancient au-
thorities. Our time is marked, as Robert Oppenheimer said in
a Columbia University address, by "the massive character of the
dissolution of authority, in belief, in ritual, and in temporal
order."

It is inevitable, in such a world, that new concerns arise. Our
art, drama, and literature, not to mention the experience of the
therapists, bear massive evidence of the feeling of disarray. The
picture of a globe overcrowded with men equipped with means
of self-destruction and lacking an assurance that there is any
meaning in being alive is not a happy one. Professor Smith
argues that the loss of life-meaning is unnatural for man; it can
cripple him in his effort to find viable solutions for the awesome
problems confronting him.

Such a situation provides an open invitation to charlatans.
The countryside is full of purveyors of pabulums of reassurance.
Honest and sensitive men are rightly repelled. Trained in critical
thinking, they spot the spurious quality of claims that fail to
meet the test of reality. This may account for the fact that
Anglo-American philosophy for a generation has turned from
the great human questions and confined itself to analysis of
cognitive meaning that can be brought within the rigorous
methods of scientific analysis. In education, researchers doggedly
pursue narrower and more manageable problems that can be
brought within the canons of scientific respectability. One need
not resort to the cheap temptation to denigrate with ridicule such
efforts, in order to raise the question, "Is it enough?"; to ask,
in effect, if the intellectual community can remain responsible
while avoiding the hazardous questions of value and meaning;
to ask it to risk ventures beyond the boundaries where scientific
techniques are readily available. Tools of analysis can play their

important role in forcing clarity, without making man timid of exploring questions that extend beyond their scope. To act otherwise makes man a victim instead of a master of the tools. The plea, simply, is that the thick, rich stream of experience not be restricted to what can be brought within the compass of valuable but partial techniques. This is not to relinquish the position that truth-claims must meet the test of inquiry. Whatever restricts the potential range of man's experience, whether it be tradition and superstition, or sophisticated methods of thought, must be resisted.

If, as Professor Smith argues, man is, indeed, condemned to meaning, the ramifications of the need are as significant for educators as for philosophers. We might well be spurred to confront this challenge—uncomfortable as it may be.

In a decade when man prepares to soar into space we need new departures of the philosophic mind. These intellectual flights will require courage and the capacity to recast problems, just as imagination and daring are required to conquer physical space. Huston Smith is willing to try such a departure. We may be grateful to him for it.

Acknowledgment

I am grateful to Arthur Wirth and Richard McAdoo for encouraging me to undertake this inquiry, to my wife Eleanor and my colleague Samuel Todes for inestimably helpful suggestions along the way, and to Mrs. Marilyn Silva for preparing the typescript for publication.

H. S.

Belmont, Massachusetts
November 1964

Condemned to Meaning

We live in a time when history appears to be rushing toward some sort of climax. New knowledge breaks over us with a force and constancy that sweeps us off our feet and keeps us from regaining them. Life's tempo quickens as if to the beat of a conductor crying, "Faster, faster . . ." With moon travel we prepare to make a pass at the infinite; with DNA we are thinking of retooling our offspring. What have we not done! What may we yet not do? If only we can keep our hands off the great thermonuclear pushbutton that would scorch the earth clean for a fresh and less humanly unreliable start, the future looks dazzling.

Or rather, it would were it not for one thing: a growing question as to whether there's any point to the whole affair. For we are witness to one of the great ironies of history: The century which (in the West) has conquered disease, erased starvation, dispensed affluence, elongated life, and educated everybody has generated, in aggregate and average, the gloomiest depiction of the human condition ever rendered. An occasional Greek wondered whether it might not

13

have been better never to have been born, but an ingrowing pessimism seems to characterize most of our writers. Almost unvaryingly they depict a world that is meaningless or absurd. Open nearly any book, enter almost any theater, and

Life is a lie, my sweet. . . . It builds green trees that ease your eyes and draw you under them. Then when you're here in the shade and you breathe in and say "Oh God, how beautiful," that's when the bird on the branch lets go his droppings and hits you on the head.[1]*

Never have men known so much while doubting that it adds up to anything; never has life been covertly so empty while overtly so full.

> Was ever an insect flying between two flowers
> Told less than we are told of what we are?

In the face of this void of meaning in our time, I take my text from the French phenomenologist Maurice Merleau-Ponty: "Because we are present to a world, we are condemned to meaning."

Having, as I had supposed, completed this little book, I chanced upon a Walter Lippmann column[2] that described so exactly the problem to which the book is addressed that it read as if written as a guest preface. "Both President Johnson and Senator Barry Goldwater," wrote Lippmann,

have said that there is discontent even among those who do not have substantial material grievances. The President spoke of the feeling that "we haven't been keeping faith. . . ." And

* See Notes for references numbered serially throughout this book.

Goldwater said that there exists a "virtual despair among the many who look beyond material success to the inner meaning of their lives. . . ."

The malady is caused, I believe, by the impact of science upon religious certainty and of technological progress upon the settled order of family, class and community. The "virtual despair" comes from being uprooted, homeless, naked, alone and unled. It comes from being lost in a universe where the meaning of life and of the social order are no longer given from on high and transmitted from the ancestors but have to be invented and discovered and experimented with, each lonely individual for himself. . . .

The poignant question, which is as yet not answered, is how, with the ancestral order dissolved and the ancient religious certainties corroded by science, the modern man can find meanings which bind his experience and engage his faculties and his passions.

This "poignant question" is the question for this book.

"The thought of John Dewey . . . has the genius and power to penetrate the intellectualized crust of ordinary philosophical expression. In Dewey's thought the meaning of experience assumes a central and thematic position in philosophy, all static conceptualizations and formalizations being pushed to one side for the sake of a return to the dynamics of meaningful experience."

—Cyril Welch

"Meaning is . . . more precious in value than is truth, and philosophy is occupied with meaning."

—John Dewey

"Because we are present to a world, we are condemned to meaning."

—Maurice Merleau-Ponty

I

Meaning in the
Academic Disciplines

ANTHROPOLOGY

In the past, every culture we know anything about was born and cradled in a crèche of meaning and nursed to maturity under its aegis. And when meaning ebbs, life declines. Certain Polynesian societies are living out this truth today. Introduced suddenly into the mechanomorphic cosmology of the modern West that seems to provide no meaningful place for their lives, they are refusing to multiply and are dying from a kind of spiritual consumption.

The regularity with which primitive man throws up myths to shield himself from the unknown—greater than the regularity with which he erects shelters to protect his body from the elements—suggests that when harassing questions of "whence" and "whither" and "why" obtrude, answers must appear or life's vagrant forces will disperse and dribble out into the sand. This hypothesis may appear emphatic, but actually it understates the case. For the history of the human mind does not begin with questions; it begins with answers under whose protective canopy questions can venture forth with impunity.

The origin of the explanatory myths which all but elicit man's questionings by providing territory into which questions can safely venture is as impenetrable as the origin of man himself. These myths are as native and indispensable to early man as his basic drives. Were they not forthcoming, man's dawning consciousness, adrift in a world of terrifying riddles, would have been crushed at birth by his fear and loneliness. As surely as his body required the in-built guidelines of instinctual drives, his embryonic psyche stood in need of immediate, reassuring solutions. So right down to today the primitive mind, where it continues to exist, answers questions before it asks them. Its tales reassure, while canalizing emotions and firming up vague spiritual overtures. In this way myth constitutes a shelter within which the mind may grow in safety while beginning to probe the import of self and world.

PSYCHOLOGY

The mytho-magical world—a world interpreted by myths that ascribed to mind an influence upon matter to a degree we would consider magical—was one of the great creations of the human mind. It provided a framework of meaning so substantial that members of the tribe were all but impacted within it. But it was inevitable that under the pressures of nascent individualism it would eventually burst. The relent-less pounding of questions cracks the cake of custom, and thereafter culture ceases to deliver to its children auto-matically, as it hands to them language—*cum lacte*—a sense of the meaning of their days.

But this does not remove their need for such meaning. Psychologists studying man in the singular and man today have been as much struck with his need for meaning as have anthropologists studying man in the aggregate and man yesterday. "The most significant psychological move-ment of our day," wrote Gordon Allport in 1959, "is exis-tentialism,"[1] and two journals of existential psychology made their appearance soon thereafter as if to validate his judgment. Ludwig Binswanger, Medard Boss, and Erwin Straus, all heavily influenced by the philosophy of Martin Heidegger, have been prime movers in the movement, but Viktor Frankl has expressed its concern for meaning most succinctly. "Man," he writes, "is dominated neither by the will-to-pleasure (Freud) nor by the will-to-power (Adler), but (by the) *will-to-meaning*. . . . his deepseated striving and struggle for a . . . meaning to his existence."[2] Herbert Fingarette, whose *Self in Transformation* is one of the most interesting recent reappraisals of psychoanalysis, reaches a similar conclusion. "The disposition to increase the mean-ingfulness of life," he writes, "is fundamental to the human being."[3] Frankl thinks the disposition is so important that every human problem is intensified by a sense of meaning-lessness or "existential vacuum"; consequently any therapy which does not deal directly with the search for meaning in its patient's life is either incomplete or misses the need entirely.

Philosophers have been even more occupied with the problem of meaning than have psychologists or anthropologists. A recent review of the subject points out that "the notorious obscurity of the word 'meaning' [has] in the past two generations provoked almost every active philosophical thinker to seek some resolution of the concept into clearer and sharper outlines."[4] But the kind of meaning that has inspired this concerted attack differs significantly from the kind we have been speaking of. The philosophers whom the author of the above quotation has in mind (as evidenced by the ones he discusses in his book) are English-speaking, analytic philosophers, and the meaning that occupies this dominant Anglo-American school wears a noticeably different guise from that which interests anthropologists and therapy-oriented psychologists.

How shall we describe this difference? It seems to come down to something like this: Whereas anthropologists and psychologists have been occupied with man's concern for the meaning of *life*—whether life as a whole or specific situations within it—analytic philosophers have been concerned with the meaning of *words*. How completely the latter half of this statement holds is evidenced by the treatise cited in the preceding paragraph. Titled *The Diversity of*

Meaning, the book was written deliberately to show "that any single theory of meanings. . . . is bound to do less than justice to the complexity of problems about meaning [because] there are . . . importantly different ways of talking about meanings and correspondingly . . . several important kinds of query about meanings."[5] But the diversity the author emphasizes turns out to be within a single camp. He is at pains to alert us to the varieties of *linguistic* meaning; nowhere does he deem it pertinent to remark—if indeed he allows—that there are kinds of meaning other than linguistic.

It has remained for Continental or existentialist-phenomenological philosophers to make this latter point. Thus, with respect to the problem of meaning, the Western philosophical world falls into halves. On the one hand are the Continental philosophers who are interested in the way meanings can inhere in life-situations; the kinship of such meanings to the kinds that interest anthropologists and psychologists is evidenced by the fact that "philosophical anthropology" and "existentialist psychology" are both Continent-originated designations. On the other hand, there are the analytic philosophers who consider meaning almost exclusively as a function of language.* Something of the feel of the

* If one counts Soviet philosophy as Western, Western philosophy divides into thirds instead of halves. Until recently Soviet philosophy has not been much concerned with either life meanings or linguistic meanings. Officially committed to dialectical materialism as *the* scientific (and hence true) philosophy, it has dismissed all other philosophies and their special preoccupations as rationalizations of bourgeois mentality. Consequently, the recent publication of *The Philosophy of Man* by the Polish philosopher Adam Schaff (London: Lawrence and Wishart, 1963) assumes importance, not only generally as marking a thaw

difference between the two schools may come through if we juxtapose a characteristic sentence from each camp. In *The Myth of Sisyphus* the Continental philosopher-novelist Albert Camus writes: "Judging whether life is or is not worth living amounts to answering the fundamental question of philosophy. . . . I therefore conclude that the meaning of life is the most urgent of questions."[6] A comparably representative sentence from the most prestigious journal of analytic philosophy reads as follows: "When philosophers attempt to say what a meaning is, they generally do so in the course of trying to make explicit what it is we say about a *word* when we specify its meaning; i.e., in the course of trying to analyze meaning-*statements*."[7]

Thus, with respect to the problem of meaning, the academic world presents us with a curious schism. Where we might most hope to find one world, in the world of the mind, we find in fact two. On one side are anthropologists, therapy-oriented psychologists, theologians, and existentialist philosophers who are on (or polarized by) the Continent and interested in philosophical anthropology. On the other side are linguists and most English-speaking or analytic philosophers. With due allowance for the vagueness of

---

in Marxist philosophical orthodoxy, but specifically for our problem of meaning by arguing that Marxists must pay more attention than they have to issues the existentialists have been raising with regard to the meaning of man's individual and personal life. The book is a symptom of a small but growing movement which might be called Marxist existentialism. Its favorite Marx is the Marx of the *Economic-Philosophic Manuscripts,* who was concerned with the problem of alienation, and its representatives tend to be more interested in the quality of individual life than in tactics of ideological class struggle.

the phrases, the former may be said to be concerned with life-meanings, the latter with language-meanings.* No iron curtain divides the two camps, but a near-vacuum does. It would be too much to describe them as locked in a cold war, but essentially accurate to describe each as giving the other the cold shoulder.

The factors that account for this split in interest among philosophers provide materials for an interesting chapter in the history of ideas, if not the sociology of knowledge. The chapter would pursue such questions as whether analytic philosophers may, consciously or unconsciously, have turned from life-meanings not only to emphasize philosophy's distinctness from theology to which she had been subservient for a millenium, but also because—what is less the case on the Continent—they have been largely ignored by men of affairs and left with students (relatively unversed in life) and one another to talk to. This could produce a vicious circle: shunned by those most involved with life, these philosophers might lapse into saying less and less about life, accepting the dominant feeling that life is not their concern and hence coming to deserve and justify this shunning. Simultaneously, English-speaking philosophers may have been attracted to linguistic meanings by the positivistic no-

---

* This distinction corresponds closely to the one noted by Michael Polanyi in his *Personal Knowledge* (Chicago: University of Chicago Press, 1958), p. 58:

"The distinction between two kinds of awareness allows us readily to acknowledge . . . two kinds of meaning. . . . We may describe the kind of meaning which a context possesses in itself as *existential,* to distinguish it especially from *denotative* or, more generally, *representative* meaning."

tion that philosophy's true function is to provide a language and logic for science, as well as the Englishman's native enjoyment of language in its own right.

But it is not history that concerns us here; it is the present and the impending future. Is it healthy for philosophy to remain divided between the entirely analytic and the entirely existential, or does the disjunction represent an updated version of Kant's "the empty and the blind"? Is it possible that America's contribution to philosophy in the balance of this century may be to capitalize on the virtues of both schools and move them into creative synthesis? Today not only philosophy, but humanistic education as a whole, stands in need of revitalization. The humanities must be opened to society-at-large as the Church was opened four centuries ago. Even on the Continent, where philosophers are (as we noted) in closer touch with men of affairs than are their counterparts in English-speaking countries, humanists are speaking only to men of letters, men still rooted in the genteel tradition. In the face of this under-relevance of the humanities as currently practiced, American philosophy may possess a unique asset in being less specialized than either British or Continental philosophy, for biology teaches that the least specialized species is the one most capable of radical advance. This suggests that American philosophy may be specially equipped for a new departure—a breakthrough into incisive relevance—if it should catch a vision of what might provoke it.

Meaning might be a good topic on which to test whether

a creative union of talents now separated by the English Channel holds promise of such a breakthrough into heightened relevance. An obvious way for American philosophy to proceed with the test would be for it to accept Continental philosophy's contention that life-situations constitute legitimate referents for meaning and then bring its British-derived analytic techniques to bear in analyzing these situations and the meanings to which they give rise.

In addition to the possibility of breaking important new ground, such a move would bring to American philosophy, which today is predominantly analytic, two more specific benefits. First, it would provide proof—needed at this juncture—that analytic philosophy is essentially a method, not a doctrine (the doctrine that meanings inhere only in language), nor a preserve (the preserve of language analysis), nor an epistemology (which has only partially outgrown its positivistic past).

The second benefit can be indicated through some words from Abraham Kaplan's chapter on "Analytic Philosophy" in his *New World of Philosophy*. The chapter begins with compliment:

There is no doubt that the broad philosophical movement which I am loosely designating as "analytic philosophy" is far and away the most influential one in the English-speaking world. In almost every American university, certainly in the British ones, philosophy has virtually come to mean just this kind of enterprise. For the younger generation of students of philosophy, at any rate, the ideas of this movement are thought to be by far the most exciting and promising.[8]

The chapter ends, however, with a criticism which for its pertinence merits quoting in full.

If I had to express in one word the defect of character that I find in analytic philosophy, it would be *remoteness*—it simply is too withdrawn from so much that I feel to be so important. It is a bracing, antiseptic air, but too rarified to make my home in. When Aristotle formulated his conception of God, the question confronted him of what God could conceivably be engaged in doing. The only activity that Aristotle found worthy of deity was what he and other philosophers were engaged in—namely, thinking; and the only subject worthy for God to think about was, naturally, thought itself. So Aristotle's God was endlessly engaged in thinking about thinking. With very little paraphrase —only replacing "thought" by "language"—this might be said of analytic philosophy as well. It is a noble enterprise, and indeed, there is something divine about it. But most of us, I believe, want a philosophy which is more—human.[9]

What more effective way for analytic philosophy to overcome its remoteness and become more humanistic than by turning part of its attention to analyzing meanings that arise directly from life-situations?

II

An Analytic Approach to Existential Meaning

An airline hostess dreams that while waiting to board her plane a passenger kicks a hole in her suitcase; she asks her psychiatrist what the dream means. A couple driving home from seeing *The Seventh Seal* find themselves absorbed in discussing what the producer wanted to get across, what the film means. Anthropologists discover that primitive peoples in widely scattered areas bury their dead in a crouching position and wonder what this fact, too consistent to be dismissed as chance, means; since the posture is that of the infant in the womb, does burial in this position express hope for regeneration? A survivor writes of his months in a Nazi concentration camp: "The question . . . was, 'Has all this suffering, this dying around us a meaning?' If not, then ultimately there is no sense in surviving." In *The Adventures of the Black Girl in Search for God*, George Bernard Shaw writes that if a person moves through life "without ever asking 'What the devil does it all mean?', he (or she) is one of those people for whom Calvin accounted by placing them in his category of the predestinately damned."

Whether the meaning such persons seek to wrest from the life-situations in question has anything substantive in common with the meaning analytic philosophers find resident in words and propositions is not at issue. Suppose for the sake of argument that they have no more in common than the dual meanings of a pun; the present inquiry would remain unaffected. For we are not trying to compose a theory of meaning which will show analytic and existential meanings to be species of a common genus. Instead we are asking (at this point in the discussion) if there is any reason why analytic *methods* cannot be brought to bear on existential meanings—defined as meanings that arise directly from concrete life-situations—however close or removed these be from the verbal meanings on which these methods are usually employed. It would seem as if, sooner or later, analytic philosophy must be driven to the task by its own principles. For if, faithful to the later Wittgenstein, analytic philosophy is committed to trying to understand "the job words do," "the roles they perform,"[1] it seems only a matter of time before it must ask what job "meaning" does when men speak—as they repeatedly do—about the meaning of life and episodes within it.

The methodological principles of analytic philosophy are precise statement, rigorous argument, careful scrutiny of detailed examples, and suspicion of premature generalizations and oversimplifications. To suppose that these principles can receive even the beginnings of adequate exemplification here would be ludicrous; the difficulties inherent in the attempt to analyze existential meanings are enough to mock a lifework, to say nothing of an occasion piece. In tackling the problem one feels as if he were sitting down, not to a fabric to study its weave, but to a heap of knotted threads which would take hundreds of hands years to untangle even if the threads were not so brittle as to break at the gentlest touch. The most that can be expected from the present discussion is the drawing of several initial distinctions. But the limitations of the discussion can double for success. Insofar as its statements are imprecise, its arguments erroneous, its examples misleading, or its generalizations excessive, to just this extent will the discussion give evidence of analytic work that needs to be done in this area. Meanwhile, if anything constructive is achieved, it will support the contention that existential meanings are not in principle inaccessible to analysis.

MEANINGS *within* LIFE AND THE MEANING *of* LIFE:
ATOMIC *versus* GLOBAL MEANING

Analysis usually begins by identifying the major parts or features of its object. An obvious distinction with which to begin the analysis of existential meaning is the distinction between meanings that derive from specific situations within life as opposed to the meaning of life as a whole.

Suppose a young man who had planned to become a doctor were drafted for a role in a community theater production for no reason more far-reaching than that he seemed to be the type for the part. Suppose further that the response from the audience and the press was spectacular; that he turned out to have a talent not only far greater than that of the other actors, some of whom were contemplating the theater as a career, but also a talent that drew him into the enterprise to the point where he felt more alive than in anything else he had heretofore undertaken. It is easy to imagine that the man in question might assess the meaning of this experience to be that he should seriously rethink his vocational intent.

In doing so he may find himself reflecting on the meaning of life as a whole. Is its purpose to make money, achieve status, enjoy oneself, derive satisfactions deeper than enjoyment, contribute to the happiness of others? The relation of partial or atomic meanings (his brush with the theater) to global meaning (the meaning of his life) invites reflection. Is it possible to assess the meaning of any experience within life without to some extent appraising life's meaning as a whole? A recent book in the history of science argues that our scientific concepts have theories built into them to such an extent that to abandon a major scientific theory without providing an alternative would be to let our concepts crumble.[2] Does the same hold for existential meanings? Do our assessments of the meaning of specific life-situations have assessments of life as a whole built into them to such as extent that to alter one involves altering the other? Are meanings within life related to the meaning of life in ways analogous to the relation between semantic and syntactic meaning in language? We shall not pursue these questions.

The point here is not to show how atomic and global meanings are related; it is to show that they are distinguishable and need at times to be considered separately.

INTRINSIC *versus* EXTRINSIC MEANING

Epileptic seizures are preceded by a distinctive brain wave pattern. Electroencephalographic monitors have been built that trigger a buzzer when they register the pattern, thus warning the epileptic wearing the monitor that a seizure is in the offing. The buzz *means* that a seizure is approaching.

Such meaning is extrinsic, for it derives from the fact that it points to something beyond itself. There are, by contrast, other meanings that are relatively self-contained, that refer primarily to themselves. An evening at the theater can be a significant, in the sense of meaningful, experience in itself; similarly, a day, a task, a friendship. The distinction is reflected in our language where "X means that Y" is idiomatic for extrinsic and "X is meaningful" for intrinsic meaning. The former bespeaks a transitive relation; the latter is intransitive, a suppressed reflexive wherein the subject is taken as its own object. As the suffix "-ful" in "meaningful" suggests, intrinsic meanings are self-complete. They indwell, each part referring only to what is present as another part. None refers to anything lacking, for nothing else is needed to make sense of the experience or episode in question. An experience is meaningful insofar as its meaning is fully filled (fulfilled) in the experience itself.

Although we are primarily engaged at this point in distinguishing different kinds of meanings, we interrupt for a passing observation about how they are related. Whereas atomic meanings can be either intrinsic or extrinsic—the presence of a boy on a basketball court could mean either that he hoped to make the team or only that he enjoyed shooting baskets—global meanings seem invariably to be intrinsic. Again, our language bears out the point. If someone were to say, "The fact that John got up in time to shoot baskets for half an hour before going to school [an atomic fact] must mean that he has decided to try out for the team," the sentence would sound completely natural. The "means that" phrase would *not* sound as natural if made to follow a global subject. To say, "Miller's life is (was) meaning*ful*," implies straightforwardly that Miller leads (led) a life of fulfillment. To say, "Miller's life *means that* . . . ," would seem like a curious way to begin. If the point to be made were that Miller's life provides evidence for a conclusion distinct from that life itself—that the good die young, for instance, or that the evil flourish like the green bay tree—we would think it clearer to say, "His life *shows that* . . ."

Obviously, intrinsic meanings will have afterglows and other repercussions that spill across arbitrarily stipulated cutoff points. But this does not compromise the fact that their meaning is basically self-contained. The epileptic's buzz derives its significance from its relation to an occurrence temporally removed from it. Not so those experiences whose meaning is intrinsic.

ARTICULATE *versus* INARTICULATE MEANING

There are meanings that can be stated in words, and others that cannot be.

As an indication of the former, we cite an autobiographical passage from Havelock Ellis' *The Dance of Life*:

It so chanced that at this time I read the "Life in Nature" of James Hinton. . . . Evidently . . . my mind had reached a stage of saturated solution which needed but the shock of the right contact to recrystallise in forms that were a revelation to me. Here evidently the right contact was applied. Hinton in his book showed himself a scientific biologist who carried the mechanistic explanation of life even further than was then usual. But he was a man of highly passionate type of intellect, and what might otherwise be formal and abstract was for him soaked in emotion. Thus, while he saw the world as an orderly mechanism, he was not content . . . to stop there and see in it nothing else. As he viewed it, the mechanism was not the mechanism of a factory, it was vital, with all the glow and warmth and beauty of life; it was, therefore, something which not only the intellect might accept, but the heart might cling to. The bearing of this conception on my state of mind is obvious. It acted with the swiftness of an electric contact; the dull aching tension was removed; the two opposing psychic tendencies were fused in delicious harmony, and my whole attitude toward the universe was changed. It was no longer an attitude of hostility and dread, but of confidence and love. My self was one with the Not-Self, my will one with the universal will. I seemed to walk in light; my feet scarcely touched the ground; I had entered a new world.

The effect of that swift revolution was permanent. At first there was a moment or two of wavering, and then the primary exaltation subsided into an attitude of calm serenity towards all those questions that had once seemed so torturing.[3]

This passage is not itself an instance of articulate meaning, but it points to such an instance. To Mr. Ellis' satisfaction, at least, the author of *The Life of Nature* had succeeded not only in catching a vision of life-in-its-world as luminously meaningful. He had succeeded in forging this vision into words.

What about meanings that cannot be verbalized? The basic fact to note is that they exist. Therapists (trying to help patients understand atomic meanings) and theologians and traditional philosophers (trying to understand global meanings) labor at articulating meanings directly; poets and myth-makers give voice to meanings indirectly. But direct and indirect articulations do not exhaust meaning's domain. There are meanings we sense but cannot say. When on the death of President Kennedy, his successor said, "We have a sense of loss too deep for words," he was not speaking in hyperbole.

Meanings fall away from words by degrees. At first remove are tacit meanings.[4] These are meanings we can sense, sometimes very vividly, without being able to put them adequately (if at all) into words. "There have been days at my home in the desert," wrote John van Druten,

days of an intense stillness, when the whole place seemed as though it were imprisoned in a crystal globe, bright with sunshine, murmurous with life: as though there were an invisible Presence standing on the threshold of one's consciousness, or of the garden—one was never quite sure which—so that one wanted to say, in a breath no louder than a whisper: "Oh, come in."[5]

Who could have said what this Presence was? There are meanings that move between lovers who understand each other without speech; meanings that settle over broken nations and vanquished leaders and all who have failed; meanings that come with age, too laden with experience to be intelligible to those who have not lived great regions of life. If we could give adequate voice to such meanings we would be poets, but if we were poets there would be deeper meanings we could not describe. For when depths are encountered, speech falters or grows dumb.

Farthest removed from articulation are meanings that exist without our being aware of them at all. The fact that there are things we know without knowing that we know them is an important recent discovery. Here are three examples. A number of nonsense syllables were shown briefly to a subject with certain of the syllables followed by an electric shock. Presently the subject anticipated shock on the sight of "shock syllables," but on being questioned he wrongly identified these syllables—clear instance of a knowing that influenced his behavior but of which he was unaware. A second example is from the work of Smith and Hendrickson.[6] They exposed the picture of a smiling face so briefly that it could not be identified, and found that unsmiling faces exposed (long enough to be identified) immediately afterwards were seen as smiling slightly. The third example is from the work of Hefferline, Keenan, and Harford. They seated subjects in reclining chairs and attached recording electrodes to various parts of their bodies, including their left thumbs, telling them that the study concerned the effects on body tension of static superimposed upon music. While the subjects relaxed and listened to tape-recorded music, the experimenters spotted for each subject a thumb position which occurred less than 20 per cent of the time. Thereafter, static was superimposed on the music except when the thumb was in that position. After an hour of such conditioning, subjects showed a marked tendency to hold their thumbs in these unnatural positions, thereby eliminating the static. But when interviewed, "all . . . still believed that they had been passive victims with respect to the onset and duration of noise, and all seemed astounded to learn that they themselves had been in control."[7]

Following Lazarus and McCleary, who coined the term "subcept" (as contrasted with "concept") to refer to things we know without knowing that we know them,[8] we shall refer to meanings that affect our lives but of which we are oblivious as "subceptual meanings."

These three levels at which meanings function—articulate, tacit, and subceptual—stand proof that meaning is layered, its strata lying at various removes from speech. But though the layers are distinct, no meaning need remain fixed at a given level. "Where id was, there shall ego be. It is reclamation work, like the draining of the Zuyder Zee."[9] We quote Freud not for his conviction that the more our psychic life becomes conscious, the better, but for his recognition that meanings can shift registers. Whether they are improved by being raised first to awareness and then to articulation we leave an open question. Sometimes they are, but not necessarily.

INDIVIDUAL *versus* GENERIC MEANING

Viktor Frankl reports that when he was taken to the concentration camp at Auschwitz a manuscript ready to be published was confiscated from his pocket. In retrospect he is convinced that his wish to write this manuscript anew was a decisive factor in enabling him to survive the ordeals which proved too much for most of his fellow-prisoners, many of whom were physically more robust than he.

This illustrates Nietzsche's contention that "he who has a *why* to live for can bear almost any *how*"; likewise Dostoevski's conviction that "the secret of man's being is not only to live but to have something to live *for*." But the *whys* for which men live differ. For Frankl it was to rewrite a manuscript; for a mother it might be to care for her child; for a Marxist it could be to hasten a revolution. Nor have we reached the limits of legitimate relativity when we admit this; we must add that meaning need not be founded on *any* sense of task. The world of the Zen Buddhist—the *sunyat*— is replete with significance, but this significance does not derive from any contribution the Zennist might make to it, for the *sunyat* is self-sufficient. W. T. Stace quotes a correspondent who felt likewise:

I think I said to you that once my life was meaningless and that now it had meaning. That was misleading if it suggested that human life has a purpose and that I now know what that purpose is. . . . On the contrary I do not believe that it has any purpose at all. As Blake put it "all life is holy" and that is enough; even the desire for more seems to me mere spiritual greed. It is enough that things are; a man who is not content with what is simply does not know what is.[10]

Given a sufficiently important *why* to live for, man can indeed bear almost any *how,* but it does not follow that no man without a *why* (in the sense of a purpose extrinsic to immediate experience) can bear his *hows* equally well. People are different, and the sources of their meanings differ correspondingly. What "rings a bell" for one may not for another, and the sum of one life's experiences are certain to add up in ways different from those of every other life.

Literary artists and biographers tend to be interested in meanings which vary from person to person and from group to group; their aims are achieved when they succeed in revealing the unique way experience shapes up inside a specific person or relationship. With comparable interests historians portray the meaning of a past epoch or historical personage. But interest in meaning does not end with such variegated depictions. In addition to the question of what life meant to Benvenuto Cellini or men living in Tang China, there is the question of the meaning of *life*—period —and of features it invariably embodies: time, history, freedom, sex, death, and the-world-as-life's-matrix. Originating as they do in experiences that men share, such meanings are generic as distinct from individual meanings that vary from person to person.

III

The Meaning of Life
in Our Time

Of the drawing of distinctions there is no end, so it becomes important at some point to stop the process deliberately. Too many distinctions befuddle as readily as too few, reducing live problems to mincemeat. The preceding chapter's distinctions are enough for present purposes. Utilizing them, we propose to turn our attention to one specific kind of existential meaning, namely, that which is intrinsic, global, generic, and articulate. What, insofar as it can be stated (rendered articulate), is the meaning of human life (global) considered in its own right (intrinsic) and as pertaining to all who live it (generic)?

Questions concerning the meaning of life as a whole seem to be a compound of two sub-questions: Is life worth living? and, What is life's purpose?—keeping in mind that (as we noted in the preceding section) "purpose" in this context need not be ulterior or extrinsic in any way that would render life instrumental. The two questions can be joined by asking: Is there a purpose, which, if realized, would render life clearly worth living?

THE "CONSTRUCTIVE" CHARACTER OF ALL ARTICULATIONS

It was difficult enough for any age to answer this question, but ours confronts it across a special barrier, namely, our awareness of the constructive (and hence relativistic) character of all knowing. This curious world that we inhabit, Thoreau once remarked, is more wonderful than convenient, and one of the inconveniences it poses for man's perception of life's meaning is the fact that his knowing is incurably finite and perspectival. If our eyes perceived different wave frequencies, the world would appear unrecognizable—even more so if our senses were tuned primarily to smell instead of to sight and sound. Similarly with our minds: were they godlike, or unsplit between conscious and subconscious, or more intuitive than reasoning, how different would be the world they would bring to view. Given this understanding of the extent to which everything we know is refracted by, and hence relative to, our idiosyncratic knowing equipment, it has ceased to be possible for us to regard any purpose we take life to have as being the purpose it possesses objectively, apart from our perception of it. Specifications of life's meaning can no longer be considered verbal reflections of the meaning that inheres in life independent of our specifyings; they are not conceptual mirror images of a meaning that lies at hand, awaiting detection and description. Strictly speaking, we cannot *find* life's meaning; to a considerable degree, at least, we must *construct* it.*

Put the matter this way: If man lived under a tinted plastic bubble and had no inkling of anything outside it, he would have no reason to doubt that the sky had, in itself, the tint his bubble imparted to it. The world view of primitive man was such a bubble. Never encountering men who lived in cultural worlds that were radically different from his own, he assumed that the meaning that pervaded his world was objective. He had not invented it; it came with life, built into the ribs of being as the skeleton on which all else hung.

We no longer see things this way. Traveled in time and space, we have come to know and convenant with men whose plastic domes are tinted otherwise than our own. Thus enlightened, we can no longer assume that the sky is, in itself, the color it appears to us. The color we see is not a mirror-image of what characterizes the world apart from us. Instead, what we see is the convergence of *something* in the world with our socio-psychophysical brand of sensing apparatus. It is in part a construct.

As with physical vision, so with spiritual. From now on it is going to be difficult for man to regard any meaning he

* Cf. Benjamin Whorf, "Sciences and Linguistics," *Technology Review*, M.I.T., XLII (April 1940): "The categories and types that we isolate from the world of phenomena we do not find there because they stare every observer in the face; on the contrary, the world is presented to us in a kaleidoscopic flux of impressions which has to be organized by our minds. . . . We cut nature up, organize it into concepts, ascribe significances as we do, largely because we are parties to an agreement to do it in this way."

secures for his life as being objectively ingrained in the nature of things. He will see it as being, at least in part, a construct. This recognition of the need for meaning to be constructed, not just appropriated, is paralleled on the personal level in current ego and existential psychology. In contrast to classical Freudianism, with its "hidden reality" approach—the source of the patient's problem is objectively *there*, buried in his past, awaiting excavation—the ego/existentialist view asserts the need for the patient to construct a responsible, future-oriented program within which his past, as newly understood, can be constructively incorporated. From this perspective the task of psychoanalysis is closer to cognition than to recognition, closer to reconstruction than to remembering. The therapeutic moment cannot be truncated from the past; but if it is genuinely therapeutic, the meaning in which the past appears must be one that never before existed. When past meanings are merely resurrected, there is no therapy, only stereotype, ritual, and compulsion. This stress on the need for continued, active construction is also the theme of current phenomenology as it speaks not to patients but to mankind at large. The problem of life is to make sense—*make,* not find—where apart from this making is nonsense.

A PROVISIONAL SOLUTION TO THE PROBLEM: KANTIANISM

The originator and most persuasive advocate of the notion that the mind constructs its experience rather than receives it passively is, of course, Kant. According to this "most philosophical head that nature has produced," we never see things as they are in themselves; we see them refracted through categories of reason and perception that are built into our make-up. We find the world ordered, and knowledge possible, because our minds are "programmed" to structure the sensuous manifold by means of specific, synthetic mental acts. Order thereby prevails, but only because we bring it into the picture. What things are like apart from our perception and cognition we can never know. Kant likened the attempt to construct a metaphysical system that would depict the world as it is in itself to the beating of wings in the void.

Much in the Kantian scheme is dubious, but its insight into the mind's initiative in organizing its experience has been impressively confirmed. Unlike the liver, which lies idle until provoked, the mind is toward its materials aggressive; it works incessantly to shape what otherwise would be inchoate fragments into patterns contributory to the goals it seeks. Gestalt psychologists have demonstrated this conclusively. Apes brought up in the dark and exposed to light only in maturity must then *learn* to see; they must develop organizing principles without which sense data merely wash over them in bewildering disarray. "Dissonance reduction" provides another example of the mind at work on its materials. Experiments show that when a mind is exposed to items that are incompatible ("cognitively dissonant") it works actively to alter its perception, understanding, or evaluation of some of the items to reduce the strain.[1] It feels impelled in one way or another to work its materials around to the point where they make sense.

Current thought about existential meaning as it con-
verges from psychiatry, anthropology, and phenomenology
bears a striking resemblance to this basically Kantian view
of natural knowledge. In neither case is the pattern that
structures our experience thought to characterize things as
they exist apart from us. Both patterns—one rendering
nature intelligible, the other rendering life intelligible—are
imposed by man. And both are imposed progressively. Just
as, according to Kant, the mind never completes its task of
applying the regulative ideas of reason to ever-wider ranges
of sensation, so too man's spirit—defined as that level of the
self where faculties distinguishable at more conscious levels
as intellect, will, and emotion interpenetrate and act in
concert—faces the unending task of perceiving meaning in
ever-widening areas of human experience.

Kant did not stop with the claim that the mind reads
order into the natural world. He went on to specify the
ways in which it does so. This leads us to ask: If our
thought about meaning has become Kantian to the point of
acknowledging it to be constructive, should we not push on
to see if there are regulative principles that govern its activity. If there are, these would betray their existence through
features that patterns of meaning invariably exemplify.

THE CATEGORIES OF MEANING

Kant found twelve ways in which the mind synthesizes its
impressions to transform chaos into coherent whole. He

called these ways in which the mind orders the disparate elements that flood in upon it "categories." Paralleling his twelve categories of judgment that render nature intelligible, there appear to be five categories of meaning which man exercises to structure his billions of life-impressions which would otherwise remain random and pointless.

1. The first is *trouble*. It varies in acuteness from vague unrest to anguish so intense as to be unbearable. It varies similarly in frequency: To some it comes as episode, while for others it is a fixture so permanent as to reduce all life to bitterness or boredom and the whole world to a bog. In guise it ranges from pain that is purely physical, through psychological neuroses, to despair in the self's deepest strata: the dark night of the soul. For the Bible, trouble is sin—a pervasive severance of man from the ground of his being, which precludes wholeness with himself and others. For the Buddha, it was *dukkha,* an unsatisfactoriness grounded in life's impermanence and dependence. Kierkegaard christened it *Angst,* the deep anxiety and unhappiness that arises from the fact that man is unable to resolve the conflicting drives and inhibitions that war in his deeply divided self. What is constant amid these varied analyses is trouble itself. Whether it comes as foulness that sucks like mire or as time's slow contractions on the hopeful heart, man is born to trouble as the sparks fly upward. The human heart is star-crossed; its tension will never completely go.

2. In their loneliness, in their lack of love and craving for it, the troubled are ever in danger of drifting to meaning's edge. But a reverse motion usually occurs. Short of having

lost its fire completely, the human spirit rises like a spark from trouble's anvil, flying upward and outward toward *hope*. Hope thereby becomes meaning's second category. The Buddha's version is so forthright as to be classic. Having impressed upon his followers that birth, old age, and death revolve like a potter's wheel, and that misery is the ruler of the world, he continues; "Nevertheless, there is, O monks, an Unborn, Unoriginated, Uncreated, Unformed. If there were not, escape from the world of the born, the originated, the created, the formed, would not be possible."

The phenomenologists have shown us that man's whole being is a being-toward; not a single psychic event, not a single experience, can be named which does not point beyond the experiencer: this is one important way in which the psyche differs from objects. Man's self-transcending vector is no metaphysical speculation; it is the first fact that a true psychological empiricism can make out. As nothing else we know, from its beginning the psyche intends beyond itself.

Intends what? On one level it is impossible to say, for just as there are as many infinities as there are dimensions, there are as many hopes as there are discontents. Those who suffer from bondage and confinement dream of freedom; those who walk in darkness see (in their mind's eye) a great light. He who groans under the weight of death and transitoriness previsions eternity; while his neighbor, distraught, restless, and riven with conflict, yearns for peace that passes understanding. The varieties of hope need to be stressed, for they show that even in its ecstatic reaches aspiration can differ from person to person, retaining a taste of the soil from which it springs. But this diversity does not undercut their common stamp of hope, the prospect of a fulfillment which, regardless of the degree to which it is realized, exceeds the present. Man's visions of the good are neither identical nor totally unalike. They enjoy a profound affinity while escaping the dull invariance that is the mark of machines, never of life. Just as a mirror reflects all forms and colors without changing its own nature, so "hope" as category reflects shades of temperaments and ideals without being restricted to any.

3. Once a goal appears, there is work to be done that the goal may be realized. So *endeavor* enters as meaning's third category.

The capacity for intentional self-transcendence is the chief attribute that divides man from the lower animals. What brought the scission was the imaginative anticipation that complex thinking makes possible. Imagination can anticipate states of affairs sharply at variance from ones that pertain, which states might nevertheless be *made* to pertain (it is seen) through effort. Once this anticipatory power appears, it turns the mind into a commuter shuttling incessantly between states of affairs that *do* exist and ones that *might*. From incoherent barkings of desire man advances to distinct speech that enables him to firm up potential states of affairs by naming them. This condenses the future more substantially in the human world, and anchors it more securely in its stream of time, than is the case in the worlds of other animals. But the transition wrenches man forever from the floating world of animal acceptance. It indentures him to the ceaseless mother-labor of creation, a constant reaching toward an ampler life. Man appears unable to succeed at any distinctively human enterprise, even business, without really trying.

4. The fourth category is *trust,* the sense of being supported by the scheme of things, the feeling that one receives from life at least as much as one gives.

One might wonder if this category is needed. Cannot meaning be wrung from hope that turns solely on one's own endeavor? The answer is no; not fundamentally or in the long run. For endeavor can itself succeed only within a matrix that supports and sustains it, and man's basic matrix is not self-made or even man-made. To believe that one can climb a rope presupposes faith in both oneself and the rope. So far we are still with man, for ropes are artifacts. But what about the hemp from which ropes are twisted? Hemp is *half* man-made; it grows as man mixes his labor with the elements: sun and rain, seed and soil. And the elements themselves? Push life in any direction and one finds it floating on a sea of "given." To have confidence in life entails confidence in the sea that sustains it. A measure of trust is hope's strict correlate.*

---

* John Dewey's phrase for such trust was natural piety. In natural piety we sense human nature as a cooperating part of a larger whole; we are aware of its support from the enveloping world that imagination feels is a universe; we know that "we are citizens of this vast world beyond ourselves" (*Art as Experience* [New York: Capricorn Books, 1958], p. 195). The opposite of this attitude—impiety—fails to realize that our actions are equally a function of other natural conditions. Impiety credits human achievements and purposes to man alone, in isolation from the world of physical nature and society. See *A Common Faith* (New Haven: Yale University Press, 1934), pp. 25-26, 53.

Beyond its minimum measure trust can increase indefinitely. As it does so it converts the image of the "given" from a ladder, on which man can climb, to an escalator that carries him upward; from water upon which he can swim, to a current that carries him forward. Faith that the world is actively on one's side, or "for one," can add enormously to life's confidence and power. It accounts for Hegelian heroism, in which the hero can withstand misunderstanding and abuse because he is confident that the World Spirit will confirm and consummate his doings. Much of communism's phenomenal appeal in this century derives from precisely this source: the assurance it gives its followers that the process of history is inexorably supporting them, that their cause is the wave of the future. The principle likewise accounts for the resonance of such lines as:

That cause can neither be lost nor stayed
Which takes its course in what God hath made,

and

. . . from the beginning the fight we were winning:
Thou, Lord, wast at our side. . . . He forgets not his own.

The opposite of trust is to see ourselves as targets of an inhuman and antihuman universe that is blindly pursuing its senseless course and gloating, without heart or brain, over the absurdity of the human predicament. It is to see ourselves against an infinitely extended and lifeless cosmos, an insignificant epiphenomenon thrown up by chance evolution on a tiny speck of cosmic dust called "Earth"—a bubble that has no destiny save to burst and be forgotten. We do not argue for the consistency of this view: it mixes feelings with insentience, hostility with indifference. But persons hold it, and when they do the universe for them ceases to be a home and becomes instead a terrifying, mechanical immensity in which thought and life have no satisfying place.

Those in whom trust runs high sense things very differently. To them it is not written in the book of fate that we receive only what we deserve. To them it seems that we all receive more than we earn, win more love than we give, and are debtors at every turn to the overflowing bounty of life.

5. The final category is *mystery.*

In common parlance the word is a polite cover for ignorance, as in a "murder mystery." There is something correct in such usage, for the word does point to an unknown factor, but the usage is so superficial as to risk denaturing the word's incisive, historic sense. For in its precise meaning "mystery" bespeaks an ignorance deeper than that which can be dispelled by information. Its proper referent is *radical* ignorance: that which we not only *do* not know but *can* not know through normal modes of cognition.

This is implied in the word's etymology. "Mystery" is derived from *muein,* meaning "closing the eyes" or "closing the mouth." The significance of "closing the mouth" is clear: It warns that mysteries cannot be stated in ordinary language because their meanings transcend the purposes and perspective within which language was devised. When Greek and Oriental mystery cults held that betrayals of their revelations constituted blasphemies that had to be

expiated by death, we misread their motive if we presume
it was merely to preserve an in-group secret. The deeper
reason was that they realized that when a mystery is trans-
lated into ordinary language, as it would have to be for the
uninitiated, it is necessarily trivialized and thereby dese-
crated.

But why "closing the eyes"? Because the principle that
applies to the organ of communication (the mouth) applies
equally to the organs of reception (the eyes). If the trans-
mundane cannot be expressed through the mundane, neither can it be perceived through it. A genuine mystery is
received through a state of mind that contradicts ordinary
awareness. Therefore, since the eyes function as a part of
normal consciousness, they must be closed to permit that
which transcends the subject-object dichotomy (which vision highlights) to break through.

Thus mystery differs in principle from a puzzle or a problem or a secret. If I am told a secret, or solve a puzzle or a
problem, its mystery departs forthwith. But mystery does
not stand in such inverse ratio to knowledge; it cannot be
exorcised by information. For it is precisely while receiving
a mystery's noetic yield that we are most aware of its mys-
teriousness. A variant of this point is the fact that there can
be a mystery of the known as well as of the unknown, an
insight that is retained in the German word for mystery,
Geheimnis, implying a mode of experiencing things that is
"most close to home." Many persons have had the experience of staring idly at a printed word and seeing it suddenly
look extremely odd, grotesque even. Something similar can

happen to any experience, even the most commonplace. A leaf, a door, an unturned stone, how ordinary—until we begin to realize how little we see of it, and how arbitrary the fraction we do see. The aeons that lie behind this simple object, the vast forces that hold it in place, the "more" it entails than we can possibly dream, and suddenly the worlds around the object begin to reel and spin, the space behind it rushes away, and that which we have known all our lives, that which is ridiculously familiar, becomes simultaneously fathomlessly mysterious.

Advanced thinkers are in an unusually propitious position today to appreciate the background of mystery within which life is set. We know more than we have ever known, only to become cognizant of how much more proportionately there is that we do not know. As if the current picture of nature's physical substratum were not bewildering, multiple, and minute enough, physicists have begun to talk of the possibility of nature being infinitely layered, so that regardless of the number of layers we fathom an infinite number will remain untouched. Sensory experience turns out to be a floating condensation on swarming undefinables. Thoughts ride on words, while words derive their meaning from language systems each of which has its own rules and no one of which is privileged. Even mathematics no longer resembles a long chain of reasoning; higher mathematics proceeds by methods that are oblique and improvised. Less and less does our knowledge resemble floodlights progressively illumining reality's stage; a more appropriate image is that of radiant nebulae separated by immense expanses of darkness. But though modern man has more reason to acknowledge the reality of mystery than did his forebears, it does not follow that he is more vividly aware of it. The great anthropologist Claude Lévi-Strauss is convinced that primitive man sensed an immense gap between his actual experience and the totality of the universe which his myths sought to signify. "The Universe," he wrote, "has signified well before one begins to know what it meant. . . . As far back as from his origin, man proposes a wholeness of the significance of which he is very embarrassed to assign allocation to a specific meaning."[2] Given the fact that awareness of mystery stretches from caveman to Einstein,* it seems well to regard it, with Rudolph Otto, as an *a priori* category of the mind.[3] Man's mind is disposed not only to rationality but also to numinous awareness. The latter issues from the deepest strata of apprehension that man possesses. Mystery is not an inference from the limitations of empirical knowledge. It is a mode of direct awareness that inference at most only triggers.†

---

* Or to Lord Kelvin, say. According to this father of the trans-Atlantic cable "We know nothing, and I am much afraid we never shall know anything but appearances; the meaning of it all, the purpose, if purpose there be, is hidden from us; of essentials, we know nothing."

† Dewey was not fond of "mystery" as a word, but he was not insensitive to the phenomenon we have described. For example, he attributes the religious feeling that accompanies intense esthetic perception to the fact that such perception introduces us "into a world beyond this world which is nevertheless the deeper reality of the world in which we live in our ordinary experiences. We are carried out beyond ourselves to find ourselves. I can see no psychological ground for such properties of an experience save that, somehow, the work of art operates to deepen and to raise to great clarity that sense of an enveloping undefined whole that accompanies every normal experience" (*Art as Experience, op. cit.,* pp. 194-195).

THE CATEGORIES IN SYNDROME

When the human spirit is in health these five categories
of meaning—trouble, hope, endeavor, trust, and mystery—
function in concert, constituting the great syndrome of
man's spiritual life. But the balance between them is pre-
carious and can easily become disturbed. Thus trouble and
hope are delicately paired: Obsession with trouble to the
neglect of hope leads to spiritual defeat, while the reverse
leaves one living in make-believe. Similarly with endeavor
and trust: To stress trust at the expense of responsibility
encourages sloth, while the reverse excess leads to the wea-
riness of the man who carries the world on his shoulders.
Too much reliance on hope and trust together, to the neglect of facing one's problems and the effort required to
extricate ourselves from them, makes a soul fatuous; while
obsession with trouble and duty can turn it to lead.

The test of adequacy is that the categories be paired. The
higher the hope, the deeper the fear; the stronger the trust,
the sterner the discipline. No logic that splits meaning in
two can be faithful to life. Dewey saw this clearly: "Poets
who have sung of despair in the midst of prosperity, and of
hope amid darkest gloom," he wrote, "have been the true
metaphysicians of nature."[4] There is only one life, and it
includes both heaven and hell; the highest goodness and the
lowest evil and all that lies between are encompassed within
it. Whatever achievements life permits come through resolv-
ing the discordant forces of light and darkness, not through
denying the existence of either. Meanwhile unless the four

paired categories assume their structure within the context of the fifth—a pervading sense of the mystery in the face of which life so palpably proceeds—they remain superficial however precisely balanced.

An alternative approach to the aetiology of the human spirit is to view the categories, not with an eye to their balance (as in the preceding paragraph), but instead in sequence (the same sequence in which the categories were introduced in the preceding section), noting this time the pathology that occurs at any stage at which development is arrested. If spirit stalls on the first category, trouble, without complementing it with hope, it stays in despair. If it moves on to hope, but refuses to acknowledge the labor needed to make the hope real, it idles in fantasy and wishful thinking. If it accepts endeavor, but not trust, it is proud and brittle, stalking the world as a stage while melodramatically stressing the self-world dichotomy that it may boast of its unconquerable soul. If it trusts, but sees no mystery, it is shallow, unendowed with the awe Goethe named as man's best feature.[5] In addition to being balanced, the categories must be complete. If their syndrome is deficient on either count it falls short of the human requirement.

BEYOND KANTIANISM

Paralleling Kant's thesis that man's mind arranges what would otherwise be amorphous impressions of the natural world into orderly patterns, we posit that man's spirit—

defined again as the level of the self where reason, will, and emotion fuse and perform in concert—molds what would otherwise be a welter of pointless life-impressions into patterns of meaning.

The chief difficulty that besets this interpretation of meaning is: If the mind thus imposes meaning upon life, does not this imply that in itself life has no meaning?

As this blunt question threatens to carry us into deep water, we shall do well to ask if we have to take it seriously. What is wrong with the notion that the meaning (purpose) of life is to create and that life is meaningful (worth living) insofar as it does so? If there is nothing wrong with this view, then the fact that man originates meaning in the world places his life in the most meaningful (worthful) position possible, for surely *ex nihilo* creation is creation's supreme variety.

Certainly there is something to this line of thought. The joy of artistic creation does spring in part from the sense that one is bringing into being meanings that otherwise would never have occurred. It is an intoxicating sensation. Turning a blank canvas into a painting is (for an adult) an experience altogether unlike the child's pastime of producing—reproducing, actually—an outline duck by connecting numbered dots in some Busytime Book. But there is another half to the story. If man likes to create and finds meaning in creating, it is equally true that he wants the meanings around which he builds his life to be more substantial, more securely rooted in things than is possible if he is their sole originator. Jean-Paul Sartre has seen this as clearly as anyone in our time. No philosopher has been more unequivocal in insisting that man's life has no meaning beyond that which he himself concocts. But it is precisely because these self-made meanings carry so little cosmic weight that man is, in Sartre's estimate, "a futile passion."

Why man wants more than self-made meanings seems clear. By himself he seems so obviously incidental in the cosmos that meanings which root in nothing more substantial than himself seem paltry. Small wonder, therefore, that he wants his meanings—not least the meaning of his life— to mesh with meanings that are more amply represented in "the scheme of things entire." Throughout the philosophy of our day, whether Heidegger's philosophy of Being, Jasper's or Heidegger's or Sartre's philosophy of Existence, or even Wittgenstein's philosophy of Language, one senses the urgency with which, explicitly or implicitly, all are concerned with man's relatedness or, as the case may be, unrelatedness to what truly *is*. Is man through any of his powers, whether of logical reasoning, feeling, intuition, will or language, *at one* with the nature of things, or is he cut off from it?

The difficult question is not *why* man wants trans-human meaning but rather: What trans-human meanings, if any, are there? We shall not be able to say much about *what* they are, but we are intensely interested in reasons for thinking they exist. We have cited the artist as evidence of the delight man takes in creating. But how is his creation to be viewed? As subjective, under the control of nothing except his own free-wheeling whims and imaginings? Or does his creation embody meanings that were in some respect latent though unperceived, as Michelangelo felt when he sensed his task to be that of liberating from the surrounding stone the Idea he had received from the Lord in heaven? Neither answer taken exclusively is satisfactory. Artists feel free, but they also feel controlled; they cannot "get away with anything" artistically. This suggests that art should be viewed as a cooperative venture in which the artist renders an interpretation of perceived meanings that in certain respects precede and exceed his personal devisings.

The point is more obvious when we consider science. We are coming to see more clearly every day the extent to which science is a human construct; the extent to which it gives us, in place of the objective, God's-eye view of nature we earlier supposed, a view so edited by human purposes, methods, and equipment as to resemble a painting (not very representational at that) more than a literal photograph. To change the image, science has come to seem more a composition played on nature's console than like a tape recording of the music of the spheres. Nevertheless, "conventionalism"—the view that science merely *prescribes* "principles of procedure" and "regulative maxims" for working with nature without *describing* nature at all— never quite makes its case. For how could we succeed so well with a nature about whose nature we know nothing? Most scientists persist in believing that their theories tell us something about properties which nature possesses in its own right, and hence that it remains more accurate to speak of discovering truth than of inventing it. Paralleling the meaning that awaits artists' perception and embodiment are truths that await scientists' discovery. Man's shadow lies *across* his science, but his science is more than that shadow.

Phenomenology appears to be moving in the direction suggested by the two preceding paragraphs. Husserl, the founder of modern phenomenology, thought (except at the very end of his life) that we *give* our experience its only meaning, but Merleau-Ponty detected a passive component in perception that constitutes a difficulty for the central Husserlian position. Merleau-Ponty accepted the gestalt psychologists as having shown that we *discover* meanings already embedded in our experience. In his Translator's Preface to *Sense and Non-Sense,* Hubert Dreyfus summarizes Merleau-Ponty's position as follows:

Thus we are not the absolute source of meaning. We do not give ready made sense *to* our experience from a transcendent position outside the world (as in Husserl), but rather we make sense *out of* our experience from within it. In Heidegger, particularly the Heidegger after *Being and Time* . . . Merleau-Ponty found a philosophical version of this view that meanings are not *given to* experience but *received from* it.[6]

What, out of all this, do we conclude for the meaning of life insofar as it is possible to discern it in our time?

Beginning with the conviction that Kant was on the right track in regarding man's mind as a pattern-making instrument, we posit a comparable propensity in the human spirit to work its life experiences into meaningful patterns exemplifying the categories of trouble, hope, endeavor, trust, and mystery. The meaning achieved through this synthetic activity can be subceptual (feeding life with courage and zest without our being aware of its existence), tacit (in which case we sense life's significance without being able to say what it is), or articulate. But though we agree with Kant that man is a meaning-maker, we do not accept the sharp form-matter dichotomy he took over from traditional philosophers, a dichotomy which led him to see order as entirely man-made. On this point Hegel, the favorite whipping boy of analytic and existential philosophers alike, was closer to the truth. Mistaken as he was about the Absolute and history's forced march toward rationality, he was nonetheless correct in denying that experience can be split into meaningless data and the form or meaning that the mind gives to this data. Meaning undercuts all dichotomies, softening them in the act.

The meaning man senses his life to possess is neither forced upon him by facts nor subjectively contrived. It exceeds the facts while taking account of them. It is neither exclusively subjective nor exclusively objective but something of each.* It emerges as man answers in continuing

---

* Awareness that subject-object dichotomies are provisional or heuristic rather than final seems to be breaking out everywhere today. Regarding knowledge generally, an important recent study argues that *"personal participation* of the knower in all acts of understanding . . . does not make our understanding *subjective.* Comprehension is neither an arbitrary act nor a passive experience, but a responsible act claiming universal validity. Such knowing is indeed *objective* in the sense of establishing contact with a hidden reality; a contact that is defined as the condition for anticipating an indeterminate range of yet unknown (and perhaps yet inconceivable) true implications. It seems reasonable to describe this fusion of the personal and the objective as Personal Knowledge" (Michael Polanyi, *Personal Knowledge, op. cit.,* pp. vii-viii).

dialogue the beckonings that come from a world that envelops us while transcending us and all that we know. The meaning does not duplicate what already existed. Just as a rocket lights up a night sea scene, so it brings novelty into an expanse of darkness. But it was prompted.

It will be protested that we have not said what life's meaning is, we have merely described how our sense of such meaning arises (when it does arise) and what we are to think is its cosmic status. This is true. The reason is that we consider articulations of life's meaning to be relative—not absolutely relative, but relative within the bounds of the categories we have described. Some men and women have no yen to have life's meaning articulated at all. We should not infer from this that meaning is unimportant for them; it is more likely that their lives are so replete with subceptual or tacit meaning that they feel no need to get it articulated. As for those who do seek to find life's meaning expressed, no single version can do service for all. To impress the soul with words—remembering that we are using "soul" and "spirit" to denote the deepest level of the self where intellect, will, and emotion converge—is tricky business. So much depends on the individual's past associations with words and images, to say nothing of his philosophy and (extremely important) his taste, his intellectual style. Put into words, one man's meaning is another man's mush; one man's passion is another man's platitude. The moral is not (as we might be tempted to infer) that it is a mistake to try to convert life's meaning into words, for if some persons do not need creeds and philosophies of life, others emphatically do. But the framing of these is a task of a different order from that upon which we have been here engaged. We are convinced that any adequate statement of life's meaning must exemplify the five categories we specified and exemplify them in syndrome. Specificity beyond this is a story for another day.

IV

Import for Education

If the foregoing thesis about meaning is in the main accurate, what is its import for education? It has implications for the curriculum and pedagogy, but we shall make no attempt to outline a rounded educational program. Instead we shall confine ourselves to a handful of issues which, though they cannot help but affect the teacher's estimate and pursuit of his vocation, lie near the foundations of his task. In the end they bear upon the deep underlying springs of the subconscious which feed both teachers' and students' intellects and their conscious lives generally.

MEANING AS A SPECIAL PROBLEM FOR OUR TIME

Education achieves most when sensitive to the social climate that surrounds it, the problems, needs, and aspirations of the society within which it functions. When this climate changes, tradition ceases to be an adequate guide for educational policy and procedure. It follows that the first need of teachers respecting meaning is to recognize that its attainment has become especially difficult at our juncture in history. Erik H. Erikson has shown that the problems of individual life differ at its various stages: During adolescence the individual faces the identity crisis (the problem of discovering who one is and wants to be); in later life the problem shifts to integrity (has one remained faithful to his self-identity?). In the same way civilizations face different problems at different stages. Although history and anthropology suggest that men have always sought meaning for their lives, since World War II Western man appears to have had unusual difficulty in finding it. It is not likely that John Dewey, were he living today, would be insensitive to this difficulty, for Dewey was nothing if not contemporary. He had an extraordinary gift for speaking relevantly to the problems of his time, being himself an outstanding exemplar of his contention that "however it may stand with philosophy as a revelation of eternal truths, it is tremendously significant as a revelation of the predicaments, protests and aspirations of humanity."[1]

In every age the human heart has had to weather stretches of winter—short, icy days and long, sharp-fanged nights. But in the past these stretches were considered seasonal. For intuitively, symbolically (through myths and rites), and rationally (as argued in philosophies and theologies) each age felt life's meaning to be secure. When the presence of this meaning ebbed, the cry was "How long, O Lord, how long," 'Why dost Thou hide thy face from us?" It was assumed the face was there.

Today we are not sure that it is. In the course of his development, writes Crane Brinton, man has been forced to abandon his most cherished myths.

He has abandoned his animism; his Ptolemaic astronomy that assured his position in the center of the universe; his faith in a hereafter that endowed him with eternal life; his belief in the supreme and infinite worth of his person that assured him a position of isolate dignity in an otherwise meaningless and impersonal world; and even perhaps his faith in a God whose attributes, under the impact of man's rationalistic scrutiny, became ever more abstract until He vanished in the metaphysical concept of the Whole. The shedding of these inestimable illusions may be merely stages in his diminishing stature before he himself vanishes from the scene—lost in the icy fixity of his final state in a posthistoric age.[2]

Being "inestimable," these historic meanings were presumably not relinquished voluntarily. What then eroded them? A combination of four developments: science, increasing contact with other cultures, rapid social change, and society's growing impersonalism.

The controlling activity of the human mind in the modern world has been science; as a consequence positive science and the autonomous intellect it enshrines has come to be regarded as reason's paradigm. But life-meanings and values slip through the methods of science (conceived in any precise sense) like sea through the nets of fishermen. Hence the more man has come to restrict his conviction to the findings of science, the more this once incurably autistic animal has had difficulty persuading himself that the universe has meaning for him at all, or that his life is more than a datum, an object of inquiry, a material for "behavioristic engineering."

If, having weaned himself of expectation that meaning is grounded in the cosmos, man turns around to look for it within the human enterprise, he is brought up short by cultural relativism. Different societies (he discovers as his contacts with them increase) have different values and meanings, each pattern of which provides a viable life-map. Like the special theory of relativity that did away with absolute space in the sense of a particular inertial system to which all natural processes are to be referred, cultural relativism appears to have done away with the notion of absolute human values and meanings. Shall man, then, resign himself to standards freely accepted as of his own society only? Social change has become too swift to permit these standards to remain stable. As a last, desperate resort the individual resolves to ground the meaning of his life in himself, only to find that the mobility of current society (which changes the residence of a typical citizen on an average of once every five years and his job three times) together with vocational specialization has so reduced his life to role-behavior—behavior in which what matters is *what* is done, not *who* is doing it—as to leave him little selfhood to build his personal meaning *on*.

It is in this context that we are to understand contemporary art. Art tends always to be the most sensitive barometer of the human spirit. Today it is typified by "The Theater of the Absurd"—"absurd" being precisely defined by the authors of this theater as not "ridiculous" but "without sense, purposeless."[3] Perhaps the first thing that strikes us about such plays as *Waiting for Godot* or *Endgame* is their use of a stark, barren stage.

It is a country of "bare ruined choirs" where we are not at all sure the sweet birds sang late or soon—or ever. Stripped of all that is familiar, comforting, prosaic, they are like the gaunt plains of the moon. An alien atmosphere for alienated men. Man cannot but be estranged from this grim environment, this universe both careless and hostile, whose obdurate mask is consonant with the blank wall dividing person from person and the individual from himself. How strange this terrain, how frighteningly empty of "the apple tree, the singing, and the gold."[4]

We are never sure of geography or chronology in these plays, for the coordinates of time and space are blurred. More shocking and disorienting, like the funhouse mirrors of amusement parks, is the absence of expected patterns of human interaction. Deprived of conventional social landmarks and recognizable roles or motivations, the characters live in a subsistence economy of the psyche. They are barely alive. Something terrible has happened to their world; it has become inhuman, while carrying memory-traces of a more normal realm. Needless to say, the plays have no plot. They are not themselves meaningless, but they depict people for whom the world is truly and ultimately "absurd." Nothing retains any real purpose, a fact most strikingly exemplified in the fact that the characters have no consequential decisions to make. If this theater seems removed from classrooms and the lives of those who people

them, Paul Goodman's *Growing Up Absurd,* Edger Fried-
enburg's *The Vanishing Adolescent,* and Andrew Greeley's
Strangers in the House point out that it is not.[5]

A number of questions are debatable. Do *Godot* and *La
Dolce Vita* exaggerate? Do Beckett and Fellini hate man or
love him too much to accept without protest his present
condition? Is our problem to learn to live creatively in the
face of meaninglessness or to try to find more meaning than
we currently perceive? We bypass these issues as ones on
which teachers can reasonably differ. What seems indis-
putable is the fact that something in the order of a crisis in
this area of meaning is upon us. Those who work with
maturing minds need to be aware of its existence and, to the
extent of their ability, its nature, for the vitality of their
students' lives, and thereby their minds, will turn to a considerable extent on the degree to which the student in question succeeds or fails to resolve the problem.

THE TEACHER'S ROLE

One of the most interesting recent experiments having
implications for education was performed by Robert Rosen-
thal.[6] He divided a large number of rats into two groups,
satisfying himself that there was no difference in their intelligence level. One group of rats he gave to half of his graduate assistants, telling them he was giving them genius rats;
the second group of rats he gave to the remaining graduate
assistants, telling them they were getting stupid rats. He then
set both groups of assistants to work teaching their rats to

run an identical maze. The resulting data showed the "genius rats" to have learned their lessons noticeably faster than did the "stupid rats."

This finding abounds with implications—some gratifying, some disturbing—for the teacher's role in learning. If his expectation can make a difference to learning across species and in circumstances where "teacher-pupil" contact was limited to the brief intervals in which the graduate assistants carried their rats from cage to maze and back, how much greater is the difference such expectations will make in contexts where pupils are in the protracted presence of teachers whose attitudes are transmitted by words, tone of voice, and face-and-body gestures rather than handling?

The school cannot be the primary source of meaning for its students, but it can be an important secondary source. Teachers can help in both specific and general ways: specifically in the way they use their minds, and generally through the influence of their total lives.

Consider first the teacher's life-impact. There is no way to insure that meaning will increase in children's lives during their school years, but the best hope for its doing so is to have them sharing time and space with teachers in whose lives meaning runs strong enough to be contagious. For ecology is actual. Man is not the skin-encapsulated entity that sight sometimes fools us into supposing. He is more like a hydra, for the sea of social forces does not just swirl around him, but washes in and through him. A classroom is a kind of weather system. Just as we take on the mood of the day, being drawn toward cheerfulness or gloom according to whether the day is sunny or overcast, so students tend to internalize the psychic climate of their schools. The chief controls in this climate are its teachers, whether they are interested or apathetic. Every society has its jaded palates and broken spirits, but unless such persons possess some exceptional talent that makes them indispensable for other reasons, they have no right to teach the young. Education is the arterial system of society and can stand only so much tired blood. The sense of meaning that should infuse it has nothing to do with the doctrinaire optimism of the public relations professional. It is compatible with soapbox Cassandras and acid iconoclasts as long as these are driven by visions of a new heaven and a new earth. What it cannot withstand is lives that have congealed in sneers or slumps.

Academia holds it fashionable to be uncommitted—a pipe-smoking, tweed-jacketed counterpart and forerunner of the beatnik. The pose is defended as being ideal for a surgical examination of truth, without personal bias. There is something to this,* but when the posture is presented to the young as an ego ideal it contributes to the pervasive malaise of modern civilization, augmenting the feeling that nothing is worthwhile, that all is a game of one-upmanship. One thinks of the suicide note: "So tired of buttoning and unbuttoning." Challenged on his critical attitude toward everything, a professor roared: "Hercules was commissioned to *clean* the Augean stables, not to refill them." Sta-

* How much and how little I have tried to indicate in "Objectivity *versus* Commitment," Chapter 3 of *The Purposes of Higher Education* (New York: Harper & Brothers, 1955).

bles need to be cleaned, but one made completely aseptic lacks life and the power to support it.

The meaning teachers impart through their zest for life is immensely important. But teachers are specialists, and the way they use their specialty—the mind—also helps or hinders students in attaining meaning.

One way in which the sharp instrument of the teacher's intellect can puncture meaning is by failing to make plain the limits of an inquiry that has produced a given finding. We know it is misleading to quote out of context, but every inquiry plucks facts from their contexts and can mislead if this is not recognized. We know the dangers of a limited sample, but every sample is limited, not only in ways sampling techniques make plain but often in other ways that are ignored, if recognized at all. So students hear of the scientific view of reality without hearing a fraction as much about the extent to which this view is conditioned by the limits of the scientific method; the extent to which science is restricted to certain kinds of answers because it asks only certain kinds of questions. Or students hear conscience reduced to conditioning, God to father-image, religion to superstition, freedom to unperceived causation, without being brought to understand the assumptions and limits of the investigations that make these equations half-truths at most. The academic mind is riddled with reductionism despite our knowledge that "nothing but" is seldom right.

Today's academic temper values correctness, the accurate application of specified rules of procedure to a limited problem. Truth conceived in the classical sense as the vision of what there is in all its fullness the university is willing to table in favor of truth-tables. But if what we have said about meaning is true—if the will-to-meaning is as important as man's drives for sex and companionship and expression, if the categories we have adduced are roughly accurate and their balance indispensable to the good life—education has not finished with any important segment of human experience until its meaning-dimension has been explored. Teachers must be "stalkers of meaning," to use Sartre's phrase. For as life lived without a sense of meaning is eviscerated, so is the intellectual approach to any problem that, in the name of objectivity, leaves out the question of its human import. Kinsey's study of "outlets" has its uses, no doubt, but our understanding of the meaning of sex in human life would be distorted if we had only the Kinseys and not the D. H. Lawrences; it would be as if the whole man had been reduced to his private parts. If the slogan, "Each to his own specialization," is raised, the answer must be: "By all means—provided it is clearly recognized that it *is* a specialization and therefore reveals only a part of what is important for depth understanding."

One of the most recently founded scholarly journals is *History of Religion,* published under the auspices of The University of Chicago. Its platform as set forth by editor Mircea Eliade in its opening issue (1961) acknowledges that hermeneutics, the study of meanings,

is . . . the least-developed aspect of our discipline. Preoccupied, and indeed often completely taken up, by their admittedly ur-

gent and indispensable work of collecting, publishing, and analyzing religious data, scholars have sometimes neglected to
study their meaning.

It goes on to assert that:

like it or not, the scholar has not finished his work when he has
reconstructed the history of a religious form or brought out its
sociological, economic or political contexts. In addition, he
must understand its meaning.

In both its appraisal of an existing deficiency and its call for
remedy, this is an exemplary statement. There is not a field
in the humanities or social sciences that could not do with
its counterpart, but we shall consider the situation only in a
single field, philosophy.

Earlier we noted that Anglo-American philosophers for
the last thirty years have confined their meaning-interest
almost entirely to language meanings, leaving life-meanings
to theologians, anthropologists, Continental philosophers,
psychiatrists, and writers. Why? There are reasons. Philosophers have a professional interest in the clarity, consistency, and justification of verbal statements, and
life-meanings do not stand up well to any of these tests.

1. Expressions of life-meanings are seldom clear, which
is why the word "expressions" is better than "statements."
Myths are more effective for conveying them than are literal propositions. Plato saw this: He began *The Republic*
with arguments but ended it with a myth. Myths have a
remarkable faculty for throwing life's multitudinous experiences into configurational perspective, but it is notoriously

difficult to translate their messages into unambiguous propositional prose. Who has succeeded in giving a definitive exegesis of the Garden of Eden story or the myth of Prometheus?

2. When attempts *are* made to obviate myth's imagery by stating life-meanings literally, the resulting propositions are likely to be paradoxical: "he that seeketh his life shall lose it"; "though He slay me, yet will I trust in Him"; reality is "a dazzling darkness," "brimming with emptiness." From the philosophical perspective to exchange ambiguity for contradiction is no great gain.

3. Suppose it were possible to state life-meanings both unambiguously and consistently; they would face a third philosophical difficulty, namely, the impossibility of demonstrating their validity. How would one propose to convince a catatonic that life is good, or Job that this is a moral universe? Even Neo-Thomists, the contemporary philosophers who place more faith in proofs for the existence of God than do any others, have become aware of the extent to which subjective conditions in the thinker affect whether he will find the proofs convincing.

4. As if this were not enough, some dimensions of meaning (as we have seen) cannot be rendered by words at all; they are tacit, composed of configurations of subcepts rather than concepts. Here Lao-tzu's dictum is final: "Those who know don't say, those who say don't know." We have just said it is usually better to speak of life-meanings as expressed rather than stated. Now we must add that tacit meanings can only be evoked or sensed. The meaning

of a life, or of life in general, can never be fully raised to articulation, tied up in a verbal package and handed from one mind to the next. Speech snatches at its fringes. Words can hint and suggest, but a life-meaning that can be exhaustively contained in them is like a portrait in marble. Instead of furthering life it imprisons its subscriber in a final creed.

To each of these criticisms by philosophers, life-meanings must plead guilty. But this only shows that the criticisms are not devastating to all the mind's endeavors.

1. With respect to clarity, we must remember Aristotle's point that in any inquiry the precisions to be expected must be in proportion to the nature of the subject in question. In mathematics an ambiguity is a mistake; but it does not follow that double-meanings are evidence of sloppiness in poetry. Indeed, one of the remaining advantages of brains over computers is their ability to handle vague ideas, ones as yet imperfectly defined. In novels and paintings the brain seems to be able to work surprisingly well with material a computer would have to reject as formless. As Norbert Wiener, the founder of cybernetics, was fond of saying, "Render unto computers the things that belong to computers, and unto man the things that belong to man."

2. As for paradox, while its presence is doubtless a sign that the thinking which makes use of it is imperfect in the sense of being something less than godlike, it does not follow that such thinking is meaningless or even careless. For if man is a transitional creature, ever in movement toward a "more" that exceeds his current capacity to comprehend; if, like the expanding universe itself, it is the destiny of his

mind always to be pouring over horizons, then frontier vision which seeks to press into current language its presentiments of this "more," which is intimated but not fully disclosed, will find itself forced toward paradox. For if the prophet does not liken the new which he wishes to proclaim to something in his hearers' experience, they will not be able to understand him, while if he simply leaves the matter there they will assume he is describing no more than the conventional. Faced with the almost impossible task of blasting minds into new registers, he contradicts; he gives and he takes away.

3. Turning to the fact that assertions concerning life's meaning cannot be verified, cannot be demonstrated to be either true or false, we have known this for a long time, but the findings of psychology regarding subcepts and tacit knowing help us to understand why. Any proposal I make regarding the meaning of life as relevant to all men faces a double difficulty respecting proof. The meaning I articulate will have originated ultimately from my tacit and subceptual intuitions, which (a) cannot be summoned for criticism or review and (b) might in any case differ from the tacit and subceptual meanings of other men, for although the categories of man's spirit are universal, their specific content as well as the degree to which they effect a balanced syndrome differs from person to person. At the most elemental level a global meaning is a gestalt of subcepts representing an immense surmise by which a human spirit throws into configurational pattern innumerable psychic bits derived from genes, its personal history, the cultural tradition

in which it participates, and who knows what else, most pieces of which it could not identify if it tried. To B, whose subcepts shape up in quite a different gestalt from A, A's formulation of life's meaning is bound to sound like a string of empty word-shells.

4. As for meanings that cannot be articulated at all, these are either subcepts pure and simple or ones that build up, pyramid-fashion, into tacit meanings. The latter are substantial enough to make their presence felt, but not sufficiently determinate to be put into words. We sense their presence at times such as those in which we feel that life is an incalculable gift but cannot say why. To pursue tacit meanings with words is like pursuing butterflies with sledge-hammers. Subceptual meanings, for their part, cannot be pursued at all, for they are not detected. They betray their presence only through that final eloquence, which, as Shakespeare said, is action.

To some these last few pages may read like capitulation to irrationalism. But the test of rationality is not a loyalty oath containing a clause stating how much of what is important in life proceeds on the conscious level. It consists in following the evidence where it leads. If things that are important go on beneath the level of consciousness, it is no credit to intelligence to blink this fact. The ideal of reason is to increase the proportion of rationality in life, not to deny or ignore portions that currently lie in its twilight zone. Admittedly there are aspects of existential meaning that are awkward for philosophy, but philosophers who decline for this reason to consider such meanings will become epigones, for one of the marks of the great philosophers was their refusal to write off any really persisting human problem. We return to the point of this section: Teachers can help with the problem of meaning both by exemplifying its presence in their lives and by seeing that the meaning-import of their subject matter is not neglected.

Unless, of course, from beginning to end we have mistaken a muddle for a problem, as Wittgenstein would say, and made much ado about what is really a pseudo-problem. But this is the point of all points about which teachers must be clear: that the problem of life-meanings is not a pseudo-problem.

NOT A PSEUDO-PROBLEM

Existential meanings *would* pose no more than pseudo-problems if it should turn out that questions about them were engendered wholly by verbal confusions or emotional disturbances or both. In such an eventuality attempts (like the present one) to confront the problem of meaning directly would be misguided, for they would attend to symptom rather than cause. Effort would more profitably be directed to language analysis to clear up the verbal confusions that were occasioning a seeming problem or to psychotherapy to ameliorate the emotional difficulties that were reflecting themselves on the conscious level in feelings of meaninglessness.

Beginning with the first possibility, verbal confusions do exist and naturally complicate existential meanings when bearing on them. But the thesis that philosophical and existential problems are occasioned wholly by such confusions, though it has been around for quite a while now, has not succeeded in making its case. It is another instance of the "nothing but" fallacy: the problems in question are nothing but verbal confusions. In the 1920's and 1930's positivists settled all kinds of awkward questions to their satisfaction simply by ruling them out of meaning's bounds, only to discover later that the questions were not meaningless at all; they had simply carried meanings the positivists had failed to perceive or countenance. Different tests are proposed today for determining which problems are genuine and which confused, but none of these tests is fool-proof or objective in the sense of being unaffected by the philosophical persuasion of the person applying it.

As for the second possibility—that when man asks questions about life's meaning he is really plagued by some unconscious psychological frustration—this is a specific instance of the general thesis that drives and emotions are what call the tunes in life, leaving the mind to tag along to reflect and rationalize these as best it can. This is an inadequate account of the mind's role. It would seem that we have repudiated faculty psychology—the view that man can be divided into compartments, such as intellect, will, and emotion—only to continue to think as if one such unisolatable faculty, the intellect, can be separated out and identified as the component that is completely passive and ineffectual in life's management.

In truth, human life is neither under reason's sovereign

control nor totally indifferent to it. Marx, Nietzsche, and Freud have convinced us of the first half of this statement; it is curious that educators of all people have to be reassured periodically that the second half is also true, that reason makes a difference. It is as if the profession were plagued by doubt as to whether its work is of any consequence. Richard Hofstadter has reminded us of a persisting strata of anti-intellectualism in American life, "a resentment and suspicion of the life of the mind and of those considered to represent it, and a disposition constantly to minimize the value of that life." There is a variant of this disposition that makes its abode in the intellect itself, using thought to discredit itself by arguing that its products are not really the work of reason at all but shaped instead by psychological and social forces of which reason is largely unaware. Ironically, this brand of anti-intellectualism roots primarily in the academic community itself.

Thoughts have consequences. It seems odd in this age of psychosomatic medicine to have to belabor the fact that what a man thinks and believes can affect his life. Here are five buttresses to thinking so.

Beginning at the level of psychological theory, Gordon Allport argues that the question of whether a person's philosophy of life can be a functionally autonomous motive instead of just a reflection of childhood conditioning or a rationalization for subconscious wishes, is the fundamental problem in motivational theory. His own view is that a philosophy of life can be an autonomous motive. "More and more," he writes, "we are coming to ascribe motivational force to cognitive conditions (cf. Festinger's 'cognitive dissonance' and Bartlett's 'effort after meaning')." It follows that the "ultimate problem" for a patient who is motivated by a distorted world view may be that world view itself, in which case "the ultimate therapeutic problem" is to help the patient to see to it that the distortions in his viewpoint are corrected.[7]

Against the backdrop of this general statement we cite three instances in which articulable meanings appear to have made a difference.

1. We earlier cited Viktor Frankl's conviction that his burning desire to rewrite a confiscated manuscript helped him to survive the ordeals of a Nazi concentration camp. The relevant point to add now is that his case was not atypical. His observations as a psychiatrist convinced him that among his fellow prisoners also it was those who found meaning for their lives and a purpose for living who were able to survive the life-tests of Dachau and Auschwitz.

2. Rock-bottom alcoholics who after ingestions of LSD were able to stay off the bottle for from six to thirty-six months comprised exactly that subgroup—one-third of the total number of those involved in the study—who interpreted their LSD experience in religious, i.e., meaning-giving, categories.

3. Synanon, the "alcoholics anonymous" of drug addicts, has been able to effect an extraordinary 80 per cent cure for its members as against the 10 per cent achieved by other methods. It is striking to note that Synanon's "philosophy" contains four of the five categories of meaning we

adduced. *Trouble* is not stated, it is assumed: no one joins Synanon unless his condition is desperate. *Hope* is emblazoned in the motto inscribed on life preservers that hang as a symbol in each Synanon house: "S. S. Hang Tough," "hang tough" being addict's slang for "Don't give up." *Trust* and *endeavor* are paired in the Synanon's creed, thus: "There comes a time in everyone's life when he arrives at the conviction . . . that though the wide universe is full of good, no kernel of nourishing corn can come to him but through his toil. . . ."[8]

Here are three instances in which articulate meanings appear to have made, or be making, a difference. It may be well to round off this brief excursus on the mind's efficacy by including a writer's description of what it feels like for an articulated meaning to take hold. Arthur Koestler admits that he became converted to Marxism because he was ripe for it and lived in a disintegrating society thirsting for faith. In so saying he reminds us that articulate meanings never really grip a life unless they tie in with factors of the self that are other than cerebral. But these factors lie latent and aimless until mobilized and integrated by a pattern of ideas.

Tired of electrons and wave-mechanics, I began for the first time to read Marx, Engels, and Lenin in earnest. By the time I had finished with Feuerbach and *State and Revolution,* something had clicked in my brain which shook me like a mental explosion. To say that one had "seen the light" is a poor description of the mental rapture which only the convert knows (regardless of what faith he has been converted to). The new light seems to pour from all directions across the skull; the whole universe falls into patter like the stray pieces of a jigsaw puzzle assembled by magic at one stroke. There is now an answer to every question, doubts and conflicts are a matter of the tortured past—a past already remote, when one had lived in dismal ignorance in the tasteless, colorless world of those who *don't know.*"⁹

If, as Marx remarked, history does not march on its head, neither does it think with its feet. The mind makes a difference, and with it the meaning it does or does not achieve. But if this insures the problem of meaning against being a pseudo-problem, why do men who are not only intelligent but sensible ignore the problem? One can only conclude that the meanings they have in mind are fatuous. Never is there shortage of this genus. Meanings are fatuous when oriented around fatuous goals like becoming the Great I Am and wearing purple and white. They are fatuous when they disrupt meaning's syndrome, weighting it in favor of its positive categories (hope and trust) at the expense of due recognition of its negative ones (trouble and the endeavor it indicates). They are pernicious when projected as compensations for human weakness—solace for the weak and fearful, crutches for the lame—or as rationalizations for unresolved childhood conflicts: the revolutionary who seeks to dethrone all father-figures for oedipal reasons. The amount of self-deception that laps around us is enough to trigger in any discerning soul the still small voice that murmurs "fiddlesticks." But we do not honor truth the less because it turns to falsehood in the mouths of fools. Why then should we permit what happens to meaning in the mouth of a Coué or power-of-positive-thinker to blind us to the fact that concern for authentic meanings is a true expression of our humanity.

The world of childhood is not necessarily happy, but it is fresh and vivid. Wordsworth's description is classic:

> There was a time when meadow, grove, and stream,
> The earth, and every common sight,
> To me did seem
> Apparell'd in celestial light,
> The glory and the freshness of a dream.

Surely the child's enormous capacity for leaning derives in large part from this fresh and fascinating face the world presents him, a face so intriguing as to all but compel overtures and exploration. The most fundamental responsibility of education is to sustain this live invitingness the world has for children, and for privileged people throughout their lives. The responsibility is not always fulfilled. Traherne thought his education dulled his interest rather than quickening it: "And so with much ado I was taught the dirty devices of the world which now I unlearn and become as a little child again."

Vividness invests the child's world primarily by virtue of its novelty. As this novelty must pass, something must take its place if the world is to continue to hold the student's interest. The prime candidate for this new factor is meaning. Random squiggles on a pad are fascinating for an infant, but in a few years the pencil marks will have to carry meaning if they are to elicit even a flicker of interest.

Learning proceeds smoothly when drawn on by interest, and interest is aroused and sustained primarily by meaning. The tie between learning and meaning is so close that at the lowest, most elemental level the two terms are synonymous: learning Greek is equivalent to grasping the meaning of its letters, words, and sentences. But at more complex levels the two phenomena are not synonymous, for we can learn a fact without seeing its significance. Obviously the motivation to learn such pointless facts is, like the capacity to remember them, minimal, the moral being that students' studies need to be sustained by a sense of the import and relevance of what they are learning. Why are we asked to learn *this?* What is its significance? From among the infinite number of things that might be engaging our attention, why this?

If the point seems obvious, the counter must be that teaching does not always give evidence that it is. A case in point is our colleges where the incursion of professionalism is decreasing student interest in many courses and fomenting a new kind of pretense. Today's college is infiltrated by teachers whose loyalty is more to their professional disciplines than to the needs of their students, and who as a consequence conduct their courses as if they were boot camps for graduate schools. If it were asked of such a course, "What is the real meaning of what is being taught?" the honest, clear-eyed answer would have to be, "It means: a means of getting into graduate school in this field, doing well there, and advancing to become a contributing member of the profession." But no undergraduate can believe in successive hours of a day or week that he is going to be a professional physicist *and* a professional philosopher *and* a professional Shakespearean scholar, etc. Yet much of today's college teaching proceeds as if all of its students were going to be all of these things and more. As Jacques Barzun has pointed out: This is bad enough for a boy; for a girl it is ridiculous. When a course is designed to be meaningful primarily for students who intend to become professionals in the field, it is certain to be less than fully meaningful for those students—the bulk—who are not taking the course in this capacity.

Students need to see the facts they learn as invested with meaning derived from the theory to which the facts relate. They need to see the import of the theory as deriving from the basic purposes and methods of the discipline that produced it. They need to understand the meaning of the discipline as deriving from its place in human life: Why did man launch such a venture, what role does it serve in his life? Underlying all, students need to sense significance in life itself. If the current of meaning is broken at any point, learning declines and slows toward a stop.

V

Conclusion

"We seek," said Lyndon B. Johnson in accepting his party's nomination for President of the United States, "a nation where the meaning of man's life can match the marvels of his labors." The words touch and resonate the hope for meaning that continues under the extroversion of American life. Every age is in some respects the best of times and the worst of times. The worst features of ours are its hyperactivity, role diffusion, and vacuity. Somehow we must tighten our hold on meaning, but the old grips are not equal to the task. Until new ones are devised it is worth recalling the conclusion R. G. Collingwood reached through his study of history: that every age in the past has produced men who were wise enough to think what had to be thought, good enough to do what had to be done, and happy enough to find life not only tolerable but attractive. And if one objects, saying, "Some men, yes, but how many?" the answer must be: "More at least than their opposite kind, or human life would long ago have vanished." What sustained them, articulated or tacit, was their sense of the worth of it all. For without this saving insight how could they have undergone the labors, or endured the shame, or faced the loneliness of their Gethsemanes or drunk their cups of hemlock? For truly, man is condemned to meaning. Without it he begins in joy and hope and ends in the shroud of doubt and defeat.

Notes

Condemned to Meaning

1. Arthur L. Kopit, *Oh, Dad, Poor Dad, Mamma's Hung You in the Closet and I'm Feelin' So Sad* (New York: Hill and Wang, 1960).
2. *New York Herald Tribune,* August 7, 1964.

I. Meaning in the Academic Disciplines

1. Preface to Viktor E. Frankl, *From Death Camp to Existentialism* (Boston: Beacon Press, 1959).
2. *The Saturday Review,* September 13, 1958, p. 20.
3. (New York: Basic Books, 1963), p. 26.
4. L. Jonathan Cohen, *The Diversity of Meaning* (New York: Herder and Herder, 1963), p. 24.
5. *Ibid.,* pp. 105-106.
6. (New York: Vintage Books, 1955), pp. v, 4.
7. W. P. Alston, "The Quest for Meanings," *Mind,* 72, No. 205 (1963), 80.

8. (New York: Vintage Books, 1963), p. 53.

9. *Ibid.,* p. 90.

II. AN ANALYTIC APPROACH TO EXISTENTIAL MEANING

1. Cf. Ludwig Wittgenstein, *Philosophical Investigations* (New York: The Macmillan Co., 1953), p. 20. "For a *large* class . . . in which we employ the word 'meaning' it can be defined thus: the meaning of a word is its use in the language."

2. N. R. Hanson, *Patterns of Discovery* (Cambridge: Cambridge University Press, 1958).

3. (Boston: Houghton Mifflin Co., 1923), pp. 215–217.

4. On tacit knowledge in general, see Michael Polanyi, "Tacit Knowing: Its Bearing on Some Problems of Philosophy," *Review of Modern Physics,* 34, No. 4 (October 1962), 601–616. Also his *Personal Knowledge,* (Chicago: University of Chicago Press, 1958), passim.

5. "One Element," *Vedanta and the West,* XIII, No. 4 (July –August, 1950), 104.

6. Smith and Hendrickson, *Acta Psychologia,* II (1955), 346. This and the preceding example are cited in Michael Polanyi, "Tacit Knowing," *op. cit.*

7. R. F. Hefferline and others, "Escape and Avoidance Conditioning in Human Subject without Their Observation of the Response," *Science,* 130 (1959), 1338–1339.

8. R. S. Lazarus and R. A. McCleary, *Journal of Personality,* 18 (1949), 171; and *Psychological Review,* 58 (1951), 113.

9. Sigmund Freud, *New Introductory Lectures on Psychoanalysis* (New York: W. W. Norton, 1933), p. 112.

10. *Mysticism and Philosphy* (Philadelphia: J. B. Lippincott Co., 1960), p. 75.

III. THE MEANING OF LIFE IN OUR TIME

1. Leon Festinger, "Cognitive Dissonance," *The Scientific American,* 207, No. 27 (October 1962), 93–102.

2. Quoted in Paul Ricoeur, *La Philosophie de la Volunté,* II, *La Symbolique du Mal,* Bk. II, Pt. II (Paris: Aubier, 1960).

3. See "The Holy [defined as *mysterium tremendum*] as an A Priori Category," Chap. XVII in *The Idea of the Holy* (New York: Oxford University Press, Galaxy Book, 1958) pp. 136–142.

4. John Dewey, *Experience and Nature* (Chicago: Open Court, 1926), pp. 116–117.

5. "Awe is the best of man: howe'er the world's
   Misprizing of the feeling would prevent us,
   Deeply we feel, once gripped, the weird Portentous."
   —*Faust,* Pt. II, Act 1, Sc. v.

6. (Evanston: Northwestern University Press, 1964).

IV. IMPORT FOR EDUCATION

1. *Philosophy and Civilization* (New York: Minton, Balch & Co., 1931), p. 6.

2. (Ed.), in *The Fate of Man* (New York: Braziller, 1961), p. 513.

3. Samuel Hirsch, "Theatre of the Absurd (Made in America)," *Journal of Social Issues,* XX, No. 1 (January 1964), 49.

4. Robert N. Wilson, "Samuel Beckett: The Social Psychology of Emptiness," *ibid.,* p. 62.

5. Also Kenneth Keniston, "Alienation and the Decline of Utopia," *The American Scholar,* 29, No. 2 (Spring 1960).

6. With Kermit L. Fode, "The Effect of Experimenter Bias on the Performance of the Albino Rat," *Behavioral Science,* VIII, No. 3 (July 1963), 183–189.

7. Rollo May (ed.), *Existentialist Psychology* (New York: Random House, 1961), p. 96.

8. *The Progressive,* XXVIII, No. 2 (February 1964), pp. 33–34.

9. In Richard Crossman (ed.), *The God That Failed* (New York: Harper & Brothers, 1949), p. 23.

Format by Katharine Sitterly
Set in Linotype Times Roman
Composed, printed and bound by The Haddon Craftsmen, Inc.
HARPER & ROW, PUBLISHERS, INCORPORATED